A SOCIETY OF

INSTANT

By

Deborah Siegel

Table of Contents

INTRODUCTION

A Society of Instant

It's certainly no secret that we live in a society with a need for speed and a taste for intolerance. Most of us still understand that faster doesn't necessarily mean better, but we're willing to settle for less in order to enjoy life more right now. For most, the art of wondering and waiting, of imagining and dreaming has been discarded for over-indulgence and quantity consumption. The reward isn't to have the best, but to have it first. Coming to the market first with a new product or service is what counts; so what if it happens to have some bugs that need to be worked out or simply ignored. In the process of wanting everything instantly, what has happened to our integrity, to the human spirit, to our values and morals?

Only time will tell, if we're willing to wait. That's the question now, isn't it? Are we willing to wait for better, to wait for gratification, to wait in order to build character and self-discipline? Research shows we are at an all-time low when it comes to our ability to wait. A study at UMass Amherst examined over six million people who frequently browse the internet. What these studies showed was the average time people were willing to wait for information on various sites was a staggering two seconds. If web designers couldn't capture viewers' attention within the first two seconds, they lost the opportunity.

Time spent in the traditional classroom or at church has now been exchanged for online education and taped sermons listened to when you're stuck in traffic. Is that really maximizing time or have we lost ourselves in a runaway society? Even something as simple as thinking, meditating, and researching have been reduced to a fleeting thought, a three-minute meditation, and searching the internet for instant information.

Decisions, actions, and values are weighed against the time it takes to achieve success. It's not far off the mark to say that time is our most precious commodity.

The best thing about time is that it plays no favorites, it is the great equalizer. No matter how instantly we want to have things, and no matter how instantly we expect things to happen, we are all slaves to the same clock. We all have only 24 hours in a day to spend. And, when it is your time to go, you won't be able to exchange or buy more time—you'll be gone in an instant. Death will also be instant, but that's one instant most of us would prefer to postpone.

Our expectations of immediacy are exhausting and have taken their toll on all of us. We may be more efficient but at what cost? How perverse that most of us continue to create an even faster rat race while, at the same time, we nostalgically crave yesterday's slower lifestyle and calmer existence Perhaps taking a few moments to examine and analyze the cause and results of our need for everything instant will help us to stop and smell the roses. So, take a few moments here to do just that. If you can't stop, make yourself slow down for a brief time to discover the benefits of waiting, of being patient, of learning perseverance and determination because you were willing to wait.

Chapter One—Instant Creates Entitlement

Throughout every stage of our lives, we witness and experience the results of a society consumed by instant gratification. Instant creates a sense of entitlement in our children, teens, young adults, middle aged, and elders.

Entitlement in Children

As a society, we are so consumed by our fast-paced lives that children are being pushed aside for our own selfish needs and wants. Children used to politely request, now they angrily demand. Why? Their brains are like little sponges, and they've learned by watching others get what they want by exhibiting the same ugly behaviors. Years back, parents could pacify their children with a vague promise of "next time" or "soon." This is no longer possible in most households where love is measured by gifts and presents.

As we move through our instant way of life, we mistakenly believe our children need everything, and they need it right now. Most parents have good intentions; they hurt when their children hurt, and so to alleviate the child's suffering they provide instant comfort and gratification. Parents provide instant compensation for their children when they have experienced a loss. In many cases the instant gratification interrupts or prohibits the learning process had the child been allowed to experience the loss. Parents who are going through a divorce feel guilty, and the result of this guilt often means a deluge of presents and special offerings to compensate for the breakup. Because the child never learns balance or appropriate behaviors, he or she simply demands more and more instant relief.

Then reality hits! Parents become unable or unwilling to keep up with the demands of their child, resulting in anger and frustration in both the child and the parents. Wanting everything instantly can be a hard task-master, irrespective of one's true needs. The need for instant gratification is not really based on need, and rarely do the people get what they are seeking. Instead, those on the merry-go-round of instant gratification just continue to feel constant dissatisfaction as they search for their next instant fix.

Entitlement in Teens

This is much like what the need for instant has created in our children, except the wants are greater, more costly, and have more dangerous consequences. Teens who are deeply impacted because they receive everything instantly typically behave as if they are entitled for an entire lifetime. This can cause difficulties in both their personal and professional lives. They often have trouble in school, finding it challenging to take the time necessary to study hard and earn good grades and almost impossible to make the natural progression to high school graduation. Many teens who feel entitled opt for the faster GED certificate, receiving a diploma in a matter of months rather than years. Unfortunately, they are usually not as prepared for college, job placement, or advanced careers when taking the fast track in their education.

If teens elect to drop out of high school to start making money instantly, their limited education and qualifications negatively impact their futures, reducing their earning potential by hundreds of thousands of dollars throughout their lifetimes. Before you know it, our instant society is made up of under-achievers who still expect everything for very little effort. It's a vicious cycle that has continued to gain momentum since the 1950s.

These teens also put a tremendous financial burden on their parents because they want and expect everything immediately. They believe they are entitled to the most expensive name brand clothes, their first cars are new and expensive models, and they persuade parents to invest in the latest electronics for their entertainment. They compete with their peers about who has the most expensive and latest material things, and all the while parents are emotionally blackmailed to provide things for their entitled teens they don't need and can't afford.

Entitlement in Young Adults

As the problem with entitlement progresses into young adults who continually seek instant gratification, they find themselves getting deeper and deeper in debt. Unable to wait and save for what they want in life, they borrow until credit cards are maxed out and loans are impossible to get because of their high debt ratio. Owning a home becomes impossible because they cannot qualify. Before you know it, these young adults have lost all control of their finances and their lives. They own very little and have put themselves in a position of being ruled by their creditors.

The entitlement cycle perpetuates itself as they create more entitled children. In fact, over the past few decades the problem of entitlement has increased so drastically that retailers have learned to speak directly to those needs, encouraging people to buy, buy, buy, with no concern about when and how they will pay.

A few days ago my friends were looking for a living room chair. They had been looking for quite some time and couldn't seem to find one that was a good fit. They decided to step up their search a bit and visit one of the more expensive furniture stores to see if perhaps something would be affordable, of good quality, and comfortable. They found the chair. They were so excited; it was perfect! A great fit, looked wonderful, looked great in their living room, and the store had it in stock so it could be delivered immediately. The only catch was that it was more money than they had planned on spending. I had to admit, the chair was beautiful and extremely comfortable, but when they told me the cost I almost fell through the floor. I could have purchased an entire living room suite for what they decided to pay for one chair. What surprised me even more was their next response. "It was more than what we wanted to pay, but we took advantage of the store credit because we deserved to have the chair and we were so tired of looking."Are you kidding me? They went into significant debt because they didn't have the patience to continue their search and the chair could be delivered immediately. Big time entitlement!

Many young adults who have been raised to believe they are entitled, who have been raised in this instant society, believe they should have the best, happiest, most fulfilling jobs or careers. If something happens on their job that is not to their liking, they are soon out there looking for other employment or a career change. It puts a strain on the companies who hire them. Our government also pays unemployment benefits to those who cannot hold a job because of their unrealistic expectations of entitlement. Who makes up the government—you and I; we're the ones paying for others' feelings of entitlement.

Entitlement in the Elderly

This type of entitlement is more emotional than any of the others, with older people playing on the feelings of their caregivers or adult children. The roles have been reversed, with the adult children acting as caregivers for their aging parents. They are expected to provide for them when, because of years of entitlement themselves, they are ill equipped to do so. The aging parents may have failed to prepare financially for their retirement and golden years, so now their children are expected to fit the bill. Unfortunately, this situation can become so tense and emotionally draining because the parent is often incapable of living alone and taking care of themselves but refuses to live anywhere else except with their adult child. The parent still feels entitled to make all the decisions for him/herself, and frequently interferes with the decisions of their child. They disapprove of the life their child has created and are unable to refrain from voicing their dissatisfaction.

Family stress can be overwhelming, especially when several generations live together in the same household. You may have teens, young adults, and an aging parent. Generations of entitlement can be so stressful when everybody wants things instantly, immediately, and totally their way. Instead of creating generations of giving, loving people, our instant society has produced angry, disillusioned humans who live in a constant state of dissatisfaction.

Chapter Two—Controlled by the Clock

A society of instant is run by the clock, controlling production in the workplace, enjoyment in our off time, and fulfillment in our personal lives. One of my associates owns a business with many hourly wage employees. In order to know the exact hours worked by his employees, he decided to install a punch clock and have everyone punch in and out each day. They also had to punch out and in for breaks and during lunch. They got two fifteen minute breaks during the day and an hour for lunch, which meant all 28 employees were using the punch clock eight times every day. Often times there would be a line at the clock for employees to punch in and out, so they began cutting their work time short in order to beat the clock.

Another requirement was that no employee have overtime unless pre-approved by their manager. So, each evening the punch clock was crowded with workers trying to punch out on time without getting overtime. In many cases, they would wait at the clock for five to ten minutes in order to punch out on time. Noticing that people were leaving their work stations early to punch out on time made my friend decide to analyze just how much time was being lost because he was such a stickler about time. The average time spent waiting to punch in and out each day was 19 minutes per employee. Nineteen minutes times 28 employees was making my friend lose almost nine hours of production time each day.

Once he accepted the fact that he was trying to control his people by the clock, and it was actually costing him almost nine hours or production time, he stopped this ridiculous behavior and so did his workers. No longer controlled by the clock, they began to work harder and produce more right up to quitting time. Not being required to punch the clock relieved the stress of what would happen if they had a few moments overtime without approval, and the entire culture of the company changed from controlling to comfort.

If you don't believe you are controlled by the clock, ask yourself this: on your day off, how many times do you look at your watch and think about what you would be doing at work right about now? It's a common thing to do; we are so preoccupied with time, that we can't stop thinking about it. Today's technology companies know how important time is to us, that's why they display the time of day across the face of their phones and on their iPads. Because watches are so important to us and we're so used to checking them to see what time it is, technology is now moving to mini-computers that are worn on our wrists.

We wake up to the clock and go to bed by the clock. I can be sitting on the sofa wide awake and notice the clock reads 10:00 p.m., and suddenly I feel sleepy. The clock displays the bedtime hour, so I'm ready for bed. Waking in the morning, I'm also controlled by the clock. I try to hit the snooze to give me a few more minutes, but the clock insists on another wake-up call. By the second buzz, I'm up and at it.

Like my friend and his company, many others run their staff by the clock. We have been trained quite well by our instant society, punching in and out like little robots. We worry if we don't make it to work on time and feel guilty when we're late coming home. Once we get home, we immediately make dinner using our instant microwaves or decide to have a rest and stop for instant takeout on the way home.

The clock is a demanding task-master, and we have given over our lives to feed its need to rule. Many live their lives wondering what it would be like to sleep in, wake up to a leisurely cup of coffee on the patio, take a relaxing shower, curl up with a book, go shopping, eat a wonderfully prepared dinner around the table with our family, go to bed when we actually feel tired, and never once look at a clock to check the time.

Chapter Three—Instant's Effect on Our Health

As we live in this fast-paced society, we must learn to deal with the additional stresses that accompany this type of lifestyle, and we all know what stress can do to our bodies and minds. Our body's reaction to stress is a natural thing and was given to us so that we could react quickly. We've turned that all around, though. Now, because we live life in the fast lane, because we must have everything right now, we put undue stress on our bodies and minds. Now we need to be protected from the very thing we have created—STRESS!

A little bit of stress is not necessarily a bad thing. It can prepare you for an exciting event in your life, and you can achieve more if you have just a bit of stress to raise your energy level, alertness, and attention. The problem is we haven't learned to flip the switch that shuts down our stress. Before we know it, our stress levels have climbed higher and higher and we've reached emergency stress level. Each small stress step that we take puts a little more strain on our bodies and minds. Like building blocks, the higher we climb the more dangerous it becomes. Before long we've reached the top of our tolerance for stress, and our world comes tumbling down.

The first signs of higher stress levels might be as simple as a headache or increased irritability. That's not so bad, so we suck it up and keep on stacking those stress blocks, right? Then we start to pick up bad habits that we hope will alleviate the stress, like eating more than we should, smoking, drinking too much, and even gambling. Of course, the only relief these bad habits provide is some temporary fun. However, along with the fun come long-term problems that take us to the next stress level. We begin to worry, and the additional anxiety causes high blood pressure, depression, insomnia, fatigue, and over-all poor general health.

Then instant takes on a whole different meaning. Suddenly because you wanted the right now lifestyle, adopting the get it while you can—you get it all right. You get anger and frustration that leads to high blood pressure and heart disease. One out of every three Americans suffer from high blood pressure, some have it so bad they are at stroke level. Eighty percent of all strokes could be prevented if that person had simply practiced a more relaxed, peaceful life where waiting and stopping to smell the roses is much more agreeable.

Not only do all these health risks take a toll on you mentally and physically, but all of us pay in this instant society. We spend billions of dollars a year on healthcare and medicine for diseases that could have been prevented or avoided altogether if those who suffer had simply learned to wait and be patient. Our instant society produced instant stress that caused instant health issues that could result in instant death.

Even if you never had severe physical issues from the need for instant, there are always some emotional and mental issues that occur. It's a proven fact, people who suffer insomnia have trouble concentrating and focusing on their jobs. Their production and performance is not as high as it could be, and then they worry about it and the cycle is self-perpetuating. It's a shame to think that we are an entire society who will never reach our full potential because we actually want to reach it right now, because we do not know how to wait for a better, more improved self.

I'm sure you have heard the shrill screams of a toddler wanting something at the store and the resulting yelling of his parent as he or she refuses to give the child what they want. Those are the actions of people who are products of an instant society. The emotional and mental stress is even greater than the physical toll of such a stress laden society. Our prisons are full of criminals who are victims themselves—victims of a society that created the very issues they put them away for having. Anger, frustration, depression, hopelessness, insomnia, and dissatisfaction can cause people to commit horrendous crimes.

We all pay in a society of instant.Since the 1970s, our prison population in America has increased by 400 percent, making it the largest in the world. Many of these criminal couldn't wait to earn money, so they took what they wanted from others. By the grace of God, that could be you spending a lifetime behind bars because you could not cope with the society in which you live. Unfortunately, our instant society has robbed us of way more than any burglar could. It has robbed us of our alienable rights. How can we pursue happiness when we are never able to achieve it, when we are on a lifelong search for it, when we cannot enjoy the happiness we already have?

Our mental institutions, hospitals, prisons, workplaces, even churches are filled with people who want happiness and want it right now. They simply don't know what to do to find happiness, so they run around in an attempt to capture a fleeting moment here and there before it is snatched away by the temptation to trade it for right now relief. The problem is our society doesn't recognize the problem. This is not an issue of what you don't know can't hurt you— just the opposite. What we don't know can kill us!

Chapter Four—Instant's Influence on Our Education

Have you ever spoken to a young adult with little to no education and asked them what they wished they could do for a career? I can guarantee you; their dream was never to be flipping burgers in a fast-food restaurant. Sure, the $8.00 an hour may have looked great when they were fifteen and living at home. However, now they find themselves stuck in a minimum wage job, and they have adult responsibilities and obligations that make it impossible to live

33

well. Because of their need for instant, they have burdened their families, themselves, and an entire nation. It is all of us who must pay for the results of our instant society.

Let's take a closer look at how this instant society has negatively impacted the education of our children. Over a million American students are added to the dropout roll every year. The ones who can stick it out often graduate with a less than desirable outcome. Three out of every four students who graduate from our public schools cannot read at grade level, and two-thirds of the graduates are not proficient in math and science. What caused this decline in our education?

Shortly after World War II, our high school graduates ranked among the best in the world. Today, when comparing those statistics with other industrialized nations, our high school graduation rate is about as low as it can go—

ranking 22 out of 27 nations. McKinsey & Company stated in a 2011 study that 44 percent of dropouts under 24 years old are jobless, and high school dropouts over 25 years old are more than three times more likely to be jobless than those with college degrees.

The alternative for high school graduates who were not college material used to be to sign up for military service. However, even that is not available to many of these young adults. Recruiters are required to give the Armed Services Vocational Aptitude Battery to all high school graduates wanting to join the military. They now say that approximately a third of those high school graduates who apply score too low and are ineligible to serve our country.

Is this really a direct result of our instant society, you might ask? Absolutely! Too many of these children needed additional help in school, but nobody was there for them. We have raised several generations of latch-key kids whose parents aren't even there when they come home from school. Both parents are working in order to pay for a home and that new car they just had to have because they couldn't wait. The American Dream has now turned into the American nightmare. Their children do not have the same opportunities as they had. For the first time in years parents do not believe their children will have a better life than the one they enjoyed.

Foreign born kids who have grown up with much less are coming to the US to take advantage of what our own children do not. We are educating them and giving them jobs over our own children because the foreigners are better prepared and more qualified. They are living better lives because they were not raised within our instant society. Instead, they learned to wait, to work, and to make the sacrifices necessary to have more later on in their lives.

It's costing corporate America an arm and a leg to train our graduates for a career. They too are looking for students who are ready to hit the ground running, but today's young adults just aren't prepared to do that. Many of them choose the university they wish to attend because of their party reputation instead of the academic standing. Or, they are recruited by the school on a sport's scholarship, graduating with scores that definitely do not reflect their capabilities. When they are ineligible for professional sports, they must then depend on their education to get them in the door of corporate America. Their education is so lacking, there is no way many of them can be successful in their chosen careers.

Now that we've talked about the students, what about the teachers? The average high school teacher in the US makes between $50,000 to $60,000 a year, depending on their subject matter, education, and experience. In order to earn at the top end of the scale, teachers must have a Master's degree or higher. Unfortunately, their earning potential in another industry or career is far greater than that of teaching, and so they move on to bigger and better opportunities. For the truly idealistic die-hards who stick with their teaching dream for a few years, over half will change their minds within the first five years.

Oh, but surely this isn't a result of our instant society, is it? Most certainly! Not only is the low salary discouraging, but the challenges of teaching in today's high schools is almost insurmountable for young, inexperienced teachers who would rather just hang it up and move into the corporate world. At least there, they may not have to put up with self-indulgent teens whose entitled personalities and family upbringing have created an angry, frustrated student. When it's so tough to teach, the qualified teachers move on, and our educational system is populated with teachers close to retirement or who are not corporate material and may not be able to properly prepare our children to be either.

The turn-around doesn't begin at the high school level. Those students are already entrenched in the "right now" rat race. It begins with the education of parents to encourage them not to accept the entitled behavior in their children. We make progress with toddlers who are not given everything they want, with elementary children who are taught patience and determination by waiting for their wants, and by high school and college students who reap the rewards of actually earning a degree that will qualify them for corporate America. We get away from this vicious cycle by paying teachers what they're worth and attracting the most qualified graduates into the teaching profession in the first place. Although it sounds discouraging, it's doable, if we desire the change enough to wait for the positive results—to stop settling for less.

Chapter Five—Settle On Less Instead Of Waiting For The Best

If this has been your moto, it's time for a turn-around, don't you think? When you settle for less even just one time, you can spiral down from there and lower yourself to a lifetime of under-achievement. Make up your mind to wait for the best, to become the best person, best worker or entrepreneur, the best parent, the best child you can be. Then, climb to the top!

Howard Schultz, owner and CEO of Starbucks, did just that. He was raised in a project developed to house the poor. Although Schultz was willing to work hard and wait for the perfect opportunity, what he wasn't willing to do was settle for less. He went to Northern Michigan University on a football scholarship, and became the CEO of Starbucks in 1987, where he grew the chain of coffee shops from 60 to 16,000. It was time for him to turn it around and become the best that he could be.

Ralph Lauren was another person who refused to settle for less. He grew up in the Bronx, N.Y. He attended college for a short while, but dropped out to join the Army. While he was employed at Brooks Brothers, he had a dream of designing men's ties. He kept picturing a world of colorful ties that would revolutionize men's fashion. Bigger, brighter, more colorful ties—that was his dream, but he had to work hard and wait for a time he thought men would be ready for his ties. That time came in 1987, when Ralph Lauren made $500,000 selling a new line of men's ties. The very next year, Polo was introduced, and Lauren was well on his way to becoming a mega-billionaire.

For both of these entrepreneurs, it wasn't about sitting back and doing nothing, waiting and hoping for life's big break to come a knockin'. No, they worked hard, prepared themselves, sacrificed, and had the perseverance and determination to march ahead because they did not feel entitled. They felt honored to have earned the opportunity to become one of the privileged few.They refused to settle for less; instead, they worked and waited for the perfect time that promised to bring out their best.

We all have better within us, but what really makes the difference is whether we are willing to make sacrifices today that promise greater returns tomorrow. Many wealthy people tell the same story. They may have had profitable careers, but didn't feel as though they had reached their best, so they continued to search for something better. They didn't settle—they searched!

Everybody's best is not equal, but it takes the same amount of effort and energy for each of us to do our best. No matter what you do, be the best, perform your best, and be happy in the fact that you are giving your best. My mother is a very wise woman, and she gave me some very good advice. She said, "Whatever you do, pretend that your name would be plastered all over the job for everybody to see. It would be like you were signing every bit of work you did. Then do that job so well that you'll be proud to have your name attached to it, that people will talk about what a wonderful job that person did. Make your performance remarkable, and you'll never have to settle for less than what you can do.

Years ago when I was going to work every morning, I used to drive my car through two school zones. Since I was traveling through about the times children were on their way to school, I observed the two adults whose job it was to escort the kids safely across the street. The first woman I saw rarely smiled. She marched halfway through the crosswalk, impatiently moving the kids quickly through. Then she would return to plop down in the chair she kept on the sidewalk until the next group of children needed her help. It was interesting to watch the children walk beside her with their heads down and their shoulders hunched over their books. They too rarely smiled or played, and they certainly didn't speak to the stern woman there. She made it known she had a job to do, and they were to get right on across the street. It wasn't that she didn't do her job and protect the kids, but she wasn't performing at her best and the children were rushed and prodded.

The second crosswalk worker was incredible. He was happy and fun, and the kids enjoyed their brief encounters with them. As one or two would be waiting for the rest of the group to catch up so they could walk across the street, they'd be talking to the crosswalk worker about their day or showing him something cool on their bikes. He took great interest in the children, obviously enjoying his work. Sometimes he would form a dance line with the children, and they would parade through the crosswalk each one holding onto the other in their dance. He was like the pied-piper of crosswalk gentlemen.

You know what I realized? I was impatient to get through the first crosswalk with the old sour face woman. I would sit there tapping my foot on the floorboard or fingers on the wheel. However, at the other crosswalk it was a different story. I always looked forward to seeing the gentleman who so enjoyed his work. He not only brought joy to his job and to the children, but I delighted in seeing him every morning. That's being your best; when others look forward to seeing you and they remember the fine job you did. The best is being enjoyable, remarkable, and memorable. Sometimes it's simply a whole lot of fun!

Chapter Six—Instant's Impact on Inventions and Investments

Let's look at inventions first. America was built on the creative nature of inventive minds. These men and women saw a need and developed ways to satisfy the need. The difficulties inventors face is that rarely does the first idea or product make it to market, and if it does it stands less of a chance to actually be a profitable concept. To be an inventor, one has to be determined, persistent, tolerant, hopeful, and most of all— patient. In many situations inventors take two steps forward and one step back, making it most challenging to invent and become the best.

If inventors had a sense of entitlement, these character traits would be nonexistent. When you believe you deserve to be successful no matter what, that "no matter what" attitude sometimes allows you to become complacent. You may say to yourself, *"Well, I'm going to be successful no matter what, so I'm going to give myself a break. I'm going to go have fun with my friends and forget about becoming the best."* That is not what I meant by being patient and waiting. No, forgetting about a commitment or giving up, even for a while, means you are procrastinating.

The thing about inventions is that it can take the work of many to make an inventor successful. Becoming your best is not an isolating endeavor. Inventors require help with designing a prototype, with a patent expert, with someone who understands the ins and outs of licensing, with marketing professionals, and with an investor. People who want instant results will never make it through the process.

There is a television program called "Shark Tank," that lets entrepreneurs and inventors present their ideas, products, or services to a group of capitalists in an attempt to entice them to invest in their invention. For many, this is not an overnight endeavor, but has been years and years in the making. It's been tried, tested, and proven to work before the show. These are people who could teach us a good deal about refusing to buy into our instant society. Some become multi-millionaires because they were willing to keep getting up after failures that would bring most to their knees. They became their best because they were nonbelievers in the power and reward of instant success. They expected an investment of time and money, and they continually moved forward even when faced with repeated failures. There are many incredible ideas and inventions, but if you expect that invention to bring immediate rewards, you'll never reach your best because you'll give up trying.

Then there are those on the other side of the coin who invest. They invest in our future and the future of our nation. Some of those investments require many years before the investors are able to reap the rewards and encourage others to become their best. And what about those who invest in their country, in its land and government? If they expected immediate returns on their investments, who would even bother? Instant isn't a word in the vocabulary of top investors. Sure, they want and expect returns, but not instantly. They're at the top because they were willing to wait, to be patient for the best return possible.

Then, of course, there is the investment we make in other people. We invest in our children's future and in our present endeavors, but believe it or not we also have an investment in our past. Where we come from, what we have learned from our past directly impacts our future. So, the investment you are making now will impact your future, even if you don't see immediate returns today. Why not make a decision to forego the need for instant, to postpone a little for tomorrow's very best? I guess you must ask yourself: *"Have I invested enough in my past to secure the best future possible?"* That answer is much more likely to be affirmative if you have refused to fall into the instant trap of grabbing the "right now" in exchange for what you could have had better tomorrow.

There is nobody more concerned about your future than you; you are responsible for your success and your failures. If you are not investing in your future by preparing today, you have decided to opt out for instant. It might be okay for now, but what happens when tomorrow comes and you are unable or still unwilling to live up to your full potential? Nobody to blame but yourself! Are you ready and willing to take the responsibility for your future? If you've joined the "I want my rewards now club," you've already received the benefits of your behavior, right? However, if you were willing to wait, to be determined to continue investing in yourself until you were ready for the best, then you'll be more than willing to take responsibility for your success, right?

I want to challenge you to invest in yourself, in your children, in your loved ones, in your job, in your values and beliefs, and take charge of your future. Resist the temptation to grab at life; instead, search for a better one, one in which you have fought the good fight and earned your success. One in which the word entitlementonly refers to a belief you used to have years ago when you were young and foolish.

Chapter Seven—Creating an Angry Instant Society

Speaking of blame; we have nobody to blame for this angry instant society but ourselves. Furthermore, nobody can heal this broken culture except those who are willing to see the truth of their contribution. As good old Dr. Phil would say, "You can't fix what you don't acknowledge." Instead of being angry that you can't have your instant reward, try getting upset with yourself for ever expecting such a thing and change your behavior. Set some long-term goals and prove to yourself that it is possible to postpone your rewards, to apply the "wait and win" rule. What do I mean by the "wait and win" rule? I thought you would never ask!

The Wait and Win Rule

Decide to make waiting a winning experience. If you've been a member of the instant society for a long time, you may need to practice the Wait and

Win Rule with the simple things at first until you build some inner strength to persevere.

For example, if you're stuck in traffic and this would normally cause you to blast your horn and swear out your window, try waiting. Play your favorite song on the radio and sing along—it's impossible to be angry when you're singing. Once you've conquered the traffic wait, move on up to a more challenging wait. Learn how to wait for your computer to boot without clicking and hissing and rolling your eyes. Or, wait for your neighbor to remove the weeds from their front yard before reporting them to your HOA. While these do not carry outstanding rewards, they begin to teach you how to wait—before you know it, traffic won't bother you so much; you'll simply enjoy a few more songs. You'll be able to give your computer time to boot while you're making yourself a cup of coffee. You and your neighbor will be able to exchange a warm greeting and a friendly wave. Don't look now, but you just experienced the Wait and Win Rule.

Once you've learned the Wait and Win Rule with the little things, you'll be able to step up to each new waiting experience with the confidence that you're going to come out the winner. Instead of being angry in an instant society, chose to use your humor to get you through. Actually, animals can teach us so much about being satisfied with ourselves today but continuing to strive for a better tomorrow. They just keep trying to be better, and they rarely let their past failures negatively affect their future attempts.

I have a German shepherd that loves to herd sheep. He competes with amazing border collies and Australian shepherds that have been herding for years that have enjoyed great success in the event. My dog is by far the slowest, has the least endurance, and is the most defeated in all the field trials in which he has competed. But he has a heart for herding and he gives it his best. Everyone at the trials encourages him and enjoys his spirit, and I am confident we have all learned from his courage and determination. He is proud to perform because he is giving it his best, even though his best is the worst of the bunch. He doesn't get angry or snippy; he doesn't give up and walk off the field. He's what I consider a champion, and I know that he will continue to win because he learns a little more each competition to wait on the sheep instead of scattering them to the far corners of the field. He is a living example of how the Wait and Win Rule works.

The lesson I'm taught each time I watch my dog herd is how important it is to enjoy the moment, to make the most of every opportunity, to never give up. There is no shame in not finishing first if you have done your best and enjoyed the journey. Every time we leave a competition I take my dog for an ice cream. He is rewarded for doing his best, and he doesn't know he didn't even place. I look at his smiling little face and know that he really has won; he has lived that day to its fullest and gets an ice cream cone to boot. It doesn't get much better than that.

That isn't the only lesson I have learned from watching my dog. He doesn't pout and get mad because he didn't win. In fact, he runs to the gate after herding expecting others to applaud his efforts. He gives so much love and appreciation for every opportunity, and he gets all that back and then some. He waits when he can but doesn't beat himself up when the excitement of the chase was too much for him to resist. He'll turn to me as if to express his regret, but soon he's back focused on his job. He works every angle, looking ahead to guide and behind to see if there is anything forgotten. Each day, I learn from him to wait and watch and that the winning comes from life's pure enjoyment.

Can you imagine how wonderful life would be if we could set aside our anger in this instant society and learn to simply appreciate each day? Success would be that much sweeter if it were earned instead of handed to us with little to no effort on our part. If we angrily blame others for our failures isn't it fair that we give them credit for our successes as well? Instead of spending days being angry over an imagined slight or a loss, expect more of yourself and hold yourself accountable for your own successes. Stop being victimized by our instant society and begin to make every moment count, to live every day as if it were the first day of a wonderful existence. Minimize your anger and you'll maximize your achievement.

Chapter Eight—From Instant to Insanity

Okay, let's pretend you couldn't resist the temptation to watch the clock, to want instant gratification, to stop and smell the roses—do you believe your life will magically improve and you'll suddenly stumble onto the treasures in life you deserve? I think not. My opinion is you're living in a fantasy world where time is your enemy. I once saw a movie that spoke to this concept.

Although I don't remember the name of the movie or the featured stars, what was amazing and scary to me was its storyline. It was a science fiction story where people in this world all began their lives with a certain amount of time. Throughout their lifetimes they could earn or buy time, but the clock was always ticking. You could give time to a loved one, but it must be done before their clock completely ran down. The world was divided into realms where the rich remained young and had plenty of time for enjoying life's simple pleasures, and the poor worked for hours on end so they could have a few more hours of life. People were not allowed to travel from one level to the next in this world without permission from the people in charge of time.

It's a fantasy that is not far from the truth. Time is always ticking, but we do have choices on how we spend it and with whom we share our time. If you are always after instant, you may be wasting today while you are thinking about how to get ahead, what you need to own or wear or drive that is better than the next guy. Your days may be spinning out of control while you work constantly, only to go to bed late and get up the next day to spend another 10-hour day at work. Your health suffers, your family suffers, and we all pick up the tab.

Then we start playing the "what if" game. What if we suddenly stepped off the merry-go-round and decided not to participate in instant gratification anymore? What if we took a day off to enjoy our family? What if we saved the money and paid cash instead of going into debt for the latest and greatest thing that we think we cannot do without? You can do that, but probably not without some adjustment—not without a little bit of crazy along the way.

Twenty years ago I decided to step off and check out for a while. I had published several books, and was currently working on two at the same time. From dusk to dawn I wrote, allowing myself only a few hours for rest and sleep. I was exhausted, burned out, and depressed. I wanted to cut back, but every time I suggested to my clients that we should slow down, they were already working up another project. The only thing I knew to do was to stop completely—to step off and stop all the projects. I can tell you that was a bit of insanity in itself.

After I finally convinced my clients that I needed to take a wellness break for a few months or perhaps even a year, and after I slept for almost two weeks solid, I came to my senses and began to question what I had done. I had a successful writing company, making incredible profits, working with wonderfully talented people, and I had just thrown it all away. I went through an identity crisis, no longer knowing what to say when people asked me what I did for a living. "Well, I'm currently sleeping," wasn't exactly impressive, and so it went until I fell into an even bigger depression than before.

I had identified so strongly with what I did, that I no longer knew who I was. If I wasn't writing, I couldn't call myself a writer. If I wasn't working, that made me a no-good, lazy bum to my way of thinking. For a few months, instead of spending my time healing and renewing my joy of writing, I spent my time running to find another career or another talent that would bring back my vigor and energy. I was looking for instant wellness, an instant new career. I thought I needed to give up the writing, but what I discovered through all the insanity was that I needed to give up the rat race.

The reason I'm sharing my experience with you is to prepare you for the temporary insanity you may feel when you decide to step off, slow down, reevaluate your life and stop expecting instant outcomes. For a while, you may feel somewhat lost and have a temporary loss of confidence. You may discover that what you really thought was bothering you wasn't what it was at all. Your anger and frustration, your depression and disappointment may have been caused because you spent a lifetime rushing and running from one thing to another and your mind and body are finally screaming for relief.

That's what living in an instant society does; it cheats you and lies to you. You can't imagine leaving the fast lane; you are not quite willing to slow down the pace. So, what's the solution to this insanity? Just slow down a little at a time— tap the brakes, if you will. Lord knows, it's difficult to stop anything cold turkey, so pull yourself back from the need for speed. If you're wound up so tight that a Cheetah's pace seems snail-like to you, it may take you a while to adjust to what normal, everyday living really feels like. Try it—you'll like it!

Chapter Nine—A Return to Restful

The body is wonderfully made, resilient and strong when given enough rest. What a great reason to return to restful. Have you ever noticed that when you've had a good sleep, when you truly feel rested, everything looks more alive, more positive? That's because we've been fooled for so long into believing that frantic is what makes us feel alive, that an over-the-top pace is what it takes to be successful in this life. That is simply a lie. We've been tricked by our own creation; tricked into thinking that we'll have time to enjoy later; right now we have to be running to something or away from something.

Because we live in an instant society, we expect instant everything—instant success, instant possessions, instant happiness, instant relief from our troubles. Unfortunately, there is no instant, only a false belief that we can obtain it. I take that back, the only thing that is instant is what could be an early demise when you get caught on that never-ending stress machine we call instant. And, don't expect instant peace when you decide you want out. You'll need to take baby steps, small little steps towards an easier lifestyle that allows time for rest and relaxation that gives you physical and emotional balance. Once you have success in the baby steps, you can experiment with a few larger strides toward greater achievement.

A word of caution, take it easy when you're finding your way back to normalcy. Just because you've stopped thinking instant, stopped expecting instant, doesn't mean the rest of society is following your lead. It's so easy to get caught up in the rat race again, so easy to lose your way when you're feeling pressured to be first. Make yourself a promise that you'll take a deep breath before rushing full-steam ahead again. When you feel yourself being pulled in several different directions by the demands of our instant society, remind yourself of all the issues you once had and refuse to participate. When others try to persuade you to keep up with the Jones's, to put things on credit, to buy now and worry later, just say no. Don't be swayed by more stuff because an instant society creates a constant need for more and more stuff. It will tell you how much you need the stuff right now, and convince you that your life will be better with more stuff. Stuff will become your God and your governing force. Before that happens—STOP!

Let me ask you, what's more important—owning stuff or having control of your life? If you create unimaginable debt, you are not in charge of your life. The banks and bill collectors will own you, and they definitely don't have your interest at heart. Why do you think the bank charges $36.00 when your checking account goes insufficient funds? It's not because they want to teach you how to wait and save so that you're more able to manage your money. No, it's because they are counting on you doing that, and they are making billions of dollars off a society whose people insist on instant gratification. They are counting on the extra revenue from your overdrafts. How sad is that?

So perhaps it is about time—about time you took charge of your life. The next time you think you cannot do without, ask yourself these ten very important questions:

Do I need this item, or do I simply want it?
Can I afford this item?

What do I expect will happen if I make myself wait?

What do I expect will happen if I don't wait?

How will I feel if I wait just a little longer?

Why is it I think I cannot do without this item?

What is influencing me to have this?

Am I being controlled by our instant society?

Will I be at peace with my decision to get this instantly?

When will I learn to say no?

The last question is the most important. When will you learn to say no, if you are always willing to allow yourself to be instantly gratified? I'll tell you the answer to that one—NEVER!

Begin denying yourself a few small things here and there and your sacrifice won't seem astronomical. Will you really feel deprived if you don't get that new pair of shoes or that new tennis racket? Perhaps you need to refocus your energy on what really feels good. Think about

71

how rewarding it will feel to have a savings account that contains more than just the minimum balance in order to remain open. Consider how great it would be to own your car free and clear, even if it isn't brand new. Let your character show your worth, not what's in your pocketbook or parked in your garage. How about making this instant decision? Decide today that you will not settle, but that you will instead wait to become the best, to enjoy life without that familiar feeling of desperation. Know that waiting doesn't have to mean doing without; it may mean doing better, having greater and enjoying more.

Conclusion—It's Time for Tolerance

When you finally are able to step back and rest, be tolerant of those who haven't discovered your secret to living a happy and satisfied life. Encourage them when you recognize that familiar face of fatigue and suffer the brunt of their anger and frustration. Be understanding of their confusion and mistaken beliefs, and share your experiences with those that are still trapped by a society of instant. It's a time for tolerance.

Show others the rewards and benefits of the Wait and Win Rule. Continue to claim the victory of a life that is your own, where you call the shots and make the rules, where you determine when and how you will spend your money. Give yourself a pat on the back when you say no to retailers who try to convince you of all the things you will be losing if you don't buy into the right now mentality.

Begin by making it a habit to wait just a short while for just a small thing, and then congratulate yourself for your vigilance. Reward yourself for the wait. It doesn't have to be something big, just a little surprise for doing well with the wait. Work the buddy system, and tell a friend or loved one your plan. Set a goal; perhaps saving some money or paying off a credit card, or saying no to a weekend trip in order to enjoy an even longer and better vacation once you've paid off your card. Be there for your friend as well, and together make a decision to stop participating in the instant.

Be sure to make your goals specific, with time frames for achievement. Even if it is as simple as not eating fast food for a week and then a month, that's a great start. Encourage your children to join in and deny themselves instant gratification for a better reward later. Expect a bit of drama in the beginning when they are first being told no, but stick to your guns. If you give in now, you may be setting them up for a lifetime of entitlement. It's time to break the pattern and live a more enjoyable, satisfying life.

Teaching yourself and your family to stop the fast pace of our instant society will make you healthier and happier. The rewards of waiting will be evident in every part of your life, from your attitude to your accomplishments; I promise you it will be worth the wait. When you backslide, just pick yourself up and correct the problem. A friend of mine recently experimented with her need for instant and failed when it came time to deny herself the purchase of a new dress for a party. She bought the dress, but by the time she got home she was feeling defeated and depressed that she hadn't been able to say no and find a suitable dress in her closet.

The heaviness she felt over purchasing the dress far outweighed her enjoyment in the purchase, so she decided to return it. She went back to the store, and then she even decided to take it one step further. She shared with the store clerk why she was forced to return this beautiful dress, and the clerk totally understood. In fact, she admitted to doing the same thing and wanting to change her spending habits as well. A few weeks later when my friend paid another trip to the mall, she dropped by the same dress shop to talk to the salesgirl. She told the girl how much she had enjoyed the party and how she had been complimented on the dress she had chosen from her closet. The salesgirl also told her story of how she had decided to save for a bigger apartment. They congratulated one another and felt a small victory. They practiced the Wait to Win Rule. My friend understood that tomorrow would bring other challenges, but she looked forward to feeling in control of those as well. Her success was sweet, and her plan to leave the need for instant behind was born.

www.ingramcontent.com/pod-product-compliance
Lightning Source LLC
Chambersburg PA
CBHW041103180526
45172CB00001B/91